TREES
& Other Poems

by Joyce Kilmer

Cherokee Publishing Company
Atlanta, Georgia

Library of Congress Cataloging-in-Publication Data

Kilmer, Joyce, 1886–1918.
    Trees & other poems.

    I. Title II. Title: Trees and other poems.
PS3521.I38T7   1982   811'.52   82-14061
ISBN: 0-87797-165-X

This book is printed on acid-free paper which conforms to the
American National Standard Z39.48-1984 *Permanence of Paper for
Printed Library Materials*. Paper that conforms to this standard's
requirements for pH, alkaline reserve and freedom from ground-
wood is anticipated to last several hundred years without significant
deterioration under normal library use and storage conditions. ∞

Manufactured in the United States of America

(Previously ISBN: 0-87797-165-X)
ISBN: 0-87797-267-2

 Cherokee Publishing Company
P O Box 1730, Marietta, Ga 30061

CONTENTS

CONTENTS

THE TWELVE-FORTY-FIVE

(For Edward J. Wheeler)

WITHIN the Jersey City shed
    The engine coughs and shakes its head,
The smoke, a plume of red and white,
Waves madly in the face of night.
And now the grave incurious stars
Gleam on the groaning hurrying cars.
Against the kind and awful reign
Of darkness, this our angry train,
A noisy little rebel, pouts
Its brief defiance, flames and shouts—
And passes on, and leaves no trace.
For darkness holds its ancient place,
Serene and absolute, the king
Unchanged, of every living thing.
The houses lie obscure and still
In Rutherford and Carlton Hill.
Our lamps intensify the dark
Of slumbering Passaic Park.
And quiet holds the weary feet

THE TWELVE-FORTY-FIVE (continued)

That daily tramp through Prospect Street.
What though we clang and clank and roar
Through all Passaic's streets?   No door
Will open, not an eye will see
Who this loud vagabond may be.
Upon my crimson cushioned seat,
In manufactured light and heat,
I feel unnatural and mean.
Outside the towns are cool and clean;
Curtained awhile from sound and sight
They take God's gracious gift of night.
The stars are watchful over them.
On Clifton as on Bethlehem
The angels, leaning down the sky,
Shed peace and gentle dreams.   And I—
I ride, I blasphemously ride
Through all the silent countryside.
The engine's shriek, the headlight's glare,
Pollute the still nocturnal air.
The cottages of Lake View sigh
And sleeping, frown as we pass by.
Why, even strident Paterson
Rests quietly as any nun.

THE TWELVE-FORTY-FIVE (continued)

Her foolish warring children keep
The grateful armistice of sleep.
For what tremendous errand's sake
Are we so blatantly awake?
What precious secret is our freight?
What king must be abroad so late?
Perhaps Death roams the hills to-night
And we rush forth to give him fight.
Or else, perhaps, we speed his way
To some remote unthinking prey.
Perhaps a woman writhes in pain
And listens—listens for the train!
The train, that like an angel sings,
The train, with healing on its wings.
Now "Hawthorne!" the conductor cries.
My neighbor starts and rubs his eyes.
He hurries yawning through the car
And steps out where the houses are.
This is the reason of our quest!
Not wantonly we break the rest
Of town and village, nor do we
Lightly profane night's sanctity.
What Love commands the train fulfills,

THE TWELVE-FORTY-FIVE (continued)

And beautiful upon the hills
Are these our feet of burnished steel.
Subtly and certainly I feel
That Glen Rock welcomes us to her
And silent Ridgewood seems to stir
And smile, because she knows the train
Has brought her children back again.
We carry people home—and so
God speeds us, wheresoe'er we go.
Hohokus, Waldwick, Allendale
Lift sleepy heads to give us hail.
In Ramsey, Mahwah, Suffern stand
Houses that wistfully demand
A father—son—some human thing
That this, the midnight train, may bring.
The trains that travel in the day
They hurry folks to work or play.
The midnight train is slow and old
But of it let this thing be told,
To its high honor be it said
It carries people home to bed.
My cottage lamp shines white and clear.
God bless the train that brought me here.

PENNIES

A FEW long-hoarded pennies in his hand
    Behold him stand;
A kilted Hedonist, perplexed and sad.
The joy that once he had,
The first delight of ownership is fled.
He bows his little head.
Ah, cruel Time, to kill
That splendid thrill!

Then in his tear-dimmed eyes
New lights arise.
He drops his treasured pennies on the ground,
They roll and bound
And scattered, rest.
Now with what zest
He runs to find his errant wealth again!

So unto men
Doth God, depriving that He may bestow.
Fame, health and money go,
But that they may, new found, be newly sweet.

PENNIES (continued)

Yea, at His feet
Sit, waiting us, to their concealment bid,
All they, our lovers, whom His Love hath hid.

Lo, comfort blooms on pain, and peace on strife,
    And gain on loss.
What is the key to Everlasting Life?
    A blood-stained Cross.

TREES

(For Mrs. Henry Mills Alden)

I THINK that I shall never see
A poem lovely as a tree.

A tree whose hungry mouth is prest
Against the earth's sweet flowing breast;

A tree that looks at God all day,
And lifts her leafy arms to pray;

A tree that may in Summer wear
A nest of robins in her hair;

Upon whose bosom snow has lain;
Who intimately lives with rain.

Poems are made by fools like me,
But only God can make a tree.

STARS

(For the Rev. James J. Daly, S. J.)

BRIGHT stars, yellow stars, flashing through
    the air,
Are you errant strands of Lady Mary's hair?
As she slits the cloudy veil and bends down
    through,
Do you fall across her cheeks and over heaven
    too?

Gay stars, little stars, you are little eyes,
Eyes of baby angels playing in the skies.
Now and then a winged child turns his merry
    face
Down toward the spinning world—what a funny
    place!

Jesus Christ came from the Cross (Christ re-
    ceive my soul!)
In each perfect hand and foot there was a bloody
    hole.

STARS (continued)

Four great iron spikes there were, red and never
    dry,
Michael plucked them from the Cross and set
    them in the sky.

Christ's Troop, Mary's Guard, God's own men,
Draw your swords and strike at Hell and strike
    again.
Every steel-born spark that flies where God's
    battles are,
Flashes past the face of God, and is a star.

OLD POETS

(For Robert Cortez Holliday)

IF I should live in a forest
  And sleep underneath a tree,
No grove of impudent saplings
  Would make a home for me.

I'd go where the old oaks gather,
  Serene and good and strong,
And they would not sigh and tremble
  And vex me with a song.

The pleasantest sort of poet
  Is the poet who's old and wise,
With an old white beard and wrinkles
  About his kind old eyes.

For these young flippertigibbets
  A-rhyming their hours away
They won't be still like honest men
  And listen to what you say.

OLD POETS (continued)

The young poet screams forever
   About his sex and his soul;
But the old man listens, and smokes his pipe,
   And polishes its bowl.

There should be a club for poets
   Who have come to seventy year.
They should sit in a great hall drinking
   Red wine and golden beer.

They would shuffle in of an evening,
   Each one to his cushioned seat,
And there would be mellow talking
   And silence rich and sweet.

There is no peace to be taken
   With poets who are young,
For they worry about the wars to be fought
   And the songs that must be sung.

But the old man knows that he's in his chair
   And that God's on His throne in the sky.
So he sits by the fire in comfort
   And he lets the world spin by.

DELICATESSEN

WHY is that wanton gossip Fame
So dumb about this man's affairs?
Why do we titter at his name
Who come to buy his curious wares?

Here is a shop of wonderment.
From every land has come a prize;
Rich spices from the Orient,
And fruit that knew Italian skies,

And figs that ripened by the sea
In Smyrna, nuts from hot Brazil,
Strange pungent meats from Germany,
And currants from a Grecian hill.

He is the lord of goodly things
That make the poor man's table gay,
Yet of his worth no minstrel sings
And on his tomb there is no bay.

DELICATESSEN (continued)

Perhaps he lives and dies unpraised,
    This trafficker in humble sweets,
Because his little shops are raised
    By thousands in the city streets.

Yet stars in greater numbers shine,
    And violets in millions grow,
And they in many a golden line
    Are sung, as every child must know.

Perhaps Fame thinks his worried eyes,
    His wrinkled, shrewd, pathetic face,
His shop, and all he sells and buys
    Are desperately commonplace.

Well, it is true he has no sword
    To dangle at his booted knees,
He leans across a slab of board,
    And draws his knife and slices cheese.

He never heard of chivalry,
    He longs for no heroic times;
He thinks of pickles, olives, tea,
    And dollars, nickles, cents and dimes.

DELICATESSEN (continued)

His world has narrow walls, it seems;
  By counters is his soul confined;
His wares are all his hopes and dreams,
  They are the fabric of his mind.

Yet—in a room above the store
  There is a woman—and a child
Pattered just now across the floor;
  The shopman looked at him and smiled.

For, once he thrilled with high romance
  And tuned to love his eager voice.
Like any cavalier of France
  He wooed the maiden of his choice.

And now deep in his weary heart
  Are sacred flames that whitely burn.
He has of Heaven's grace a part
  Who loves, who is beloved in turn.

And when the long day's work is done,
  (How slow the leaden minutes ran!)
Home, with his wife and little son,
  He is no huckster, but a man!

DELICATESSEN (continued)

And there are those who grasp his hand,
   Who drink with him and wish him well.
O in no drear and lonely land
   Shall he who honors friendship dwell.

And in his little shop, who knows
   What bitter games of war are played?
Why, daily on each corner grows
   A foe to rob him of his trade.

He fights, and for his fireside's sake;
   He fights for clothing and for bread:
The lances of his foemen make
   A steely halo round his head.

He decks his window artfully,
   He haggles over paltry sums.
In this strange field his war must be
   And by such blows his triumph comes.

What if no trumpet sounds to call
   His armed legions to his side?
What if, to no ancestral hall
   He comes in all a victor's pride?

DELICATESSEN (continued)

The scene shall never fit the deed.
  Grotesquely wonders come to pass.
The fool shall mount an Arab steed
  And Jesus ride upon an ass.

This man has home and child and wife
  And battle set for every day.
This man has God and love and life;
  These stand, all else shall pass away.

O Carpenter of Nazareth,
  Whose mother was a village maid,
Shall we, Thy children, blow our breath
  In scorn on any humble trade?

Have pity on our foolishness
  And give us eyes, that we may see
Beneath the shopman's clumsy dress
  The splendor of humanity!

SERVANT GIRL AND GROCER'S BOY

HER lips' remark was: "Oh, you kid!"
Her soul spoke thus (I know it did):

"O king of realms of endless joy,
My own, my golden grocer's boy,

I am a princess forced to dwell
Within a lonely kitchen cell,

While you go dashing through the land
With loveliness on every hand.

Your whistle strikes my eager ears
Like music of the choiring spheres.

The mighty earth grows faint and reels
Beneath your thundering wagon wheels.

How keenly, perilously sweet
To cling upon that swaying seat!

SERVANT GIRL AND GROCER'S BOY (cont.)

How happy she who by your side
May share the splendors of that ride!

Ah, if you will not take my hand
And bear me off across the land,

Then, traveller from Arcady,
Remain awhile and comfort me.

What other maiden can you find
So young and delicate and kind?"

Her lips' remark was: "Oh, you kid!"
Her soul spoke thus (I know it did).

WEALTH

(For Aline)

FROM what old ballad, or from what rich
frame
Did you descend to glorify the earth?
Was it from Chaucer's singing book you came?
Or did Watteau's small brushes give you birth?

Nothing so exquisite as that slight hand
Could Raphael or Leonardo trace.
Nor could the poets know in Fairyland
The changing wonder of your lyric face.

I would possess a host of lovely things,
But I am poor and such joys may not be.
So God who lifts the poor and humbles kings
Sent loveliness itself to dwell with me.

MARTIN

WHEN I am tired of earnest men,
　　Intense and keen and sharp and clever,
Pursuing fame with brush or pen
　　Or counting metal disks forever,
Then from the halls of Shadowland
　　Beyond the trackless purple sea
Old Martin's ghost comes back to stand
　　Beside my desk and talk to me.

Still on his delicate pale face
　　A quizzical thin smile is showing,
His cheeks are wrinkled like fine lace,
　　His kind blue eyes are gay and glowing.
He wears a brilliant-hued cravat,
　　A suit to match his soft grey hair,
A rakish stick, a knowing hat,
　　A manner blithe and debonair.

How good that he who always knew
　　That being lovely was a duty,
Should have gold halls to wander through
　　And should himself inhabit beauty.

MARTIN (continued)

How like his old unselfish way
  To leave those halls of splendid mirth
And comfort those condemned to stay
  Upon the dull and sombre earth.

Some people ask: "What cruel chance
  Made Martin's life so sad a story?"
Martin? Why, he exhaled romance,
  And wore an overcoat of glory.
A fleck of sunlight in the street,
  A horse, a book, a girl who smiled,
Such visions made each moment sweet
  For this receptive ancient child.

Because it was old Martin's lot
  To be, not make, a decoration,
Shall we then scorn him, having not
  His genius of appreciation?
Rich joy and love he got and gave;
  His heart was merry as his dress;
Pile laurel wreaths upon his grave
  Who did not gain, but was, success!

THE APARTMENT HOUSE

SEVERE against the pleasant arc of sky
　　The great stone box is cruelly displayed.
　　The street becomes more dreary from its
　　　　shade,
And vagrant breezes touch its walls and die.
Here sullen convicts in their chains might lie,
　　Or slaves toil dumbly at some dreary trade.
　　How worse than folly is their labor made
Who cleft the rocks that this might rise on high!

Yet, as I look, I see a woman's face
　　Gleam from a window far above the street.
This is a house of homes, a sacred place,
　　By human passion made divinely sweet.
How all the building thrills with sudden grace
　　Beneath the magic of Love's golden feet!

AS WINDS THAT BLOW AGAINST A STAR

(For Aline)

NOW by what whim of wanton chance
    Do radiant eyes know sombre days?
And feet that shod in light should dance
    Walk weary and laborious ways?

But rays from Heaven, white and whole,
    May penetrate the gloom of earth;
And tears but nourish, in your soul,
    The glory of celestial mirth.

The darts of toil and sorrow, sent
    Against your peaceful beauty, are
As foolish and as impotent
    As winds that blow against a star.

ST. LAURENCE

WITHIN the broken Vatican
    The murdered Pope is lying dead.
The soldiers of Valerian
  Their evil hands are wet and red.

Unarmed, unmoved, St. Laurence waits,
  His cassock is his only mail.
The troops of Hell have burst the gates,
  But Christ is Lord, He shall prevail.

They have encompassed him with steel,
  They spit upon his gentle face,
He smiles and bleeds, nor will reveal
  The Church's hidden treasure-place.

Ah, faithful steward, worthy knight,
  Well hast thou done. Behold thy fee!
Since thou hast fought the goodly fight
  A martyr's death is fixed for thee.

ST. LAURENCE (continued)

St. Laurence, pray for us to bear
The faith which glorifies thy name.
St. Laurence, pray for us to share
The wounds of Love's consuming flame.

TO A YOUNG POET WHO KILLED HIMSELF

WHEN you had played with life a space
    And made it drink and lust and sing,
You flung it back into God's face
    And thought you did a noble thing.
"Lo, I have lived and loved," you said,
    "And sung to fools too dull to hear me.
Now for a cool and grassy bed
    With violets in blossom near me."

Well, rest is good for weary feet,
    Although they ran for no great prize;
And violets are very sweet,
    Although their roots are in your eyes.
But hark to what the earthworms say
    Who share with you your muddy haven:
"The fight was on—you ran away.
    You are a coward and a craven.

"The rug is ruined where you bled;
    It was a dirty way to die!
To put a bullet through your head
    And make a silly woman cry!

TO A YOUNG POET WHO KILLED HIMSELF
(continued)

You could not vex the merry stars
   Nor make them heed you, dead or living.
Not all your puny anger mars
   God's irresistible forgiving.

"Yes, God forgives and men forget,
   And you're forgiven and forgotten.
You might be gaily sinning yet
   And quick and fresh instead of rotten.
And when you think of love and fame
   And all that might have come to pass,
Then don't you feel a little shame?
   And don't you think you were an ass?"

MEMORIAL DAY

"Dulce et decorum est"

THE bugle echoes shrill and sweet,
   But not of war it sings to-day.
The road is rhythmic with the feet
   Of men-at-arms who come to pray.

The roses blossom white and red
   On tombs where weary soldiers lie;
Flags wave above the honored dead
   And martial music cleaves the sky.

Above their wreath-strewn graves we kneel,
   They kept the faith and fought the fight.
Through flying lead and crimson steel
   They plunged for Freedom and the Right.

May we, their grateful children, learn
   Their strength, who lie beneath this sod,
Who went through fire and death to earn
   At last the accolade of God.

MEMORIAL DAY (continued)

In shining rank on rank arrayed
    They march, the legions of the Lord;
He is their Captain unafraid,
    The Prince of Peace . . . Who brought a
    sword.

THE ROSARY

NOT on the lute, nor harp of many strings
  Shall all men praise the Master of all song.
Our life is brief, one saith, and art is long;
And skilled must be the laureates of kings.
Silent, O lips that utter foolish things!
  Rest, awkward fingers striking all notes wrong!
  How from your toil shall issue, white and
    strong,
Music like that God's chosen poet sings?

There is one harp that any hand can play,
  And from its strings what harmonies arise!
There is one song that any mouth can say,—
  A song that lingers when all singing dies.
When on their beads our Mother's children pray
  Immortal music charms the grateful skies.

VISION

(For Aline)

HOMER, they tell us, was blind and could
    not see the beautiful faces
    Looking up into his own and reflecting the joy
        of his dream,
    Yet did he seem
Gifted with eyes that could follow the gods to
    their holiest places.

I have no vision of gods, not of Eros with love-
    arrows laden,
    Jupiter thundering death or of Juno his white-
    breasted queen,
    Yet have I seen
All of the joy of the world in the innocent heart
    of a maiden.

TO CERTAIN POETS

NOW is the rhymer's honest trade
A thing for scornful laughter made.

The merchant's sneer, the clerk's disdain,
These are the burden of our pain.

Because of you did this befall,
You brought this shame upon us all.

You little poets mincing there
With women's hearts and women's hair!

How sick Dan Chaucer's ghost must be
To hear you lisp of "Poesie"!

A heavy-handed blow, I think,
Would make your veins drip scented ink.

You strut and smirk your little while
So mildly, delicately vile!

TO CERTAIN POETS (continued)

Your tiny voices mock God's wrath,
You snails that crawl along His path!

Why, what has God or man to do
With wet, amorphous things like you?

This thing alone you have achieved:
Because of you, it is believed

That all who earn their bread by rhyme
Are like yourselves, exuding slime.

Oh, cease to write, for very shame,
Ere all men spit upon our name!

Take up your needles, drop your pen,
And leave the poet's craft to men!

LOVE'S LANTERN

(For Aline)

BECAUSE the road was steep and long
  And through a dark and lonely land,
God set upon my lips a song
  And put a lantern in my hand.

Through miles on weary miles of night
  That stretch relentless in my way
My lantern burns serene and white,
  An unexhausted cup of day.

O golden lights and lights like wine,
  How dim your boasted splendors are.
Behold this little lamp of mine;
  It is more starlike than a star!

ST. ALEXIS

Patron of Beggars

WE who beg for bread as we daily tread
   Country lane and city street,
Let us kneel and pray on the broad highway
   To the saint with the vagrant feet.
Our altar light is a buttercup bright,
   And our shrine is a bank of sod,
But still we share St. Alexis' care,
   The Vagabond of God.

They gave him a home in purple Rome
   And a princess for his bride,
But he rowed away on his wedding day
   Down the Tiber's rushing tide.
And he came to land on the Asian strand
   Where the heathen people dwell;
As a beggar he strayed and he preached and
     prayed
   And he saved their souls from hell.

ST. ALEXIS (continued)

Bowed with years and pain he came back again
   To his father's dwelling place.
There was none to see who this tramp might be,
   For they knew not his bearded face.
But his father said, "Give him drink and bread
   And a couch underneath the stair."
So Alexis crept to his hole and slept.
   But he might not linger there.

For when night came down on the seven-hilled
      town,
   And the emperor hurried in,
Saying, "Lo, I hear that a saint is near
   Who will cleanse us of our sin,"
Then they looked in vain where the saint had lain,
   For his soul had fled afar,
From his fleshly home he had gone to roam
   Where the gold-paved highways are.

We who beg for bread as we daily tread
   Country lane and city street,
Let us kneel and pray on the broad highway
   To the saint with the vagrant feet.

ST. ALEXIS (continued)

Our altar light is a buttercup bright,
   And our shrine is a bank of sod,
But still we share St. Alexis' care,
   The Vagabond of God!

FOLLY

(For A. K. K.)

WHAT distant mountains thrill and glow
    Beneath our Lady Folly's tread?
Why has she left us, wise in woe,
    Shrewd, practical, uncomforted?
We cannot love or dream or sing,
    We are too cynical to pray,
There is no joy in anything
    Since Lady Folly went away.

Many a knight and gentle maid,
    Whose glory shines from years gone by,
Through ignorance was unafraid
    And as a fool knew how to die.
Saint Folly rode beside Jehanne
    And broke the ranks of Hell with her,
And Folly's smile shone brightly on
    Christ's plaything, Brother Juniper.

Our minds are troubled and defiled
    By study in a weary school.

FOLLY (continued)

O for the folly of the child!
The ready courage of the fool!
Lord, crush our knowledge utterly
And make us humble, simple men;
And cleansed of wisdom, let us see
Our Lady Folly's face again.

MADNESS

(For Sara Teasdale)

THE lonely farm, the crowded street,
  The palace and the slum,
Give welcome to my silent feet
  As, bearing gifts, I come.

Last night a beggar crouched alone,
  A ragged helpless thing;
I set him on a moonbeam throne—
  Today he is a king.

Last night a king in orb and crown
  Held court with splendid cheer;
Today he tears his purple gown
  And moans and shrieks in fear.

Not iron bars, nor flashing spears,
  Not land, nor sky, nor sea,
Nor love's artillery of tears
  Can keep mine own from me.

MADNESS (continued)

Serene, unchanging, ever fair,
   I smile with secret mirth
And in a net of mine own hair
   I swing the captive earth.

POETS

VAIN is the chiming of forgotten bells
 That the wind sways above a ruined
  shrine.
Vainer his voice in whom no longer dwells
 Hunger that craves immortal Bread and Wine.

Light songs we breathe that perish with our
  breath
 Out of our lips that have not kissed the rod.
They shall not live who have not tasted death.
 They only sing who are struck dumb by God.

CITIZEN OF THE WORLD

NO longer of Him be it said
    "He hath no place to lay His head."

In every land a constant lamp
Flames by His small and mighty camp.

There is no strange and distant place
That is not gladdened by His face.

And every nation kneels to hail
The Splendour shining through Its veil.

Cloistered beside the shouting street,
Silent, He calls me to His feet.

Imprisoned for His love of me
He makes my spirit greatly free.

And through my lips that uttered sin
The King of Glory enters in.

TO A BLACKBIRD AND HIS MATE
WHO DIED IN THE SPRING

(For Kenton)

AN iron hand has stilled the throats
 That throbbed with loud and rhythmic glee
And dammed the flood of silver notes
 That drenched the world in melody.
The blosmy apple boughs are yearning
For their wild choristers' returning,
 But no swift wings flash through the tree.

Ye that were glad and fleet and strong,
 Shall Silence take you in her net?
And shall Death quell that radiant song
 Whose echo thrills the meadow yet?
Burst the frail web about you clinging
And charm Death's cruel heart with singing
 Till with strange tears his eyes are wet.

The scented morning of the year
 Is old and stale now ye are gone.
No friendly songs the children hear
 Among the bushes on the lawn.

TO A BLACKBIRD AND HIS MATE WHO DIED IN THE SPRING (continued)

When babies wander out a-Maying
Will ye, their bards, afar be straying?
   Unhymned by you, what is the dawn?

Nay, since ye loved ye cannot die.
   Above the stars is set your nest.
Through Heaven's fields ye sing and fly
   And in the trees of Heaven rest.
And little children in their dreaming
Shall see your soft black plumage gleaming
   And smile, by your clear music blest.

THE FOURTH SHEPHERD

(For Thomas Walsh)

I

ON nights like this the huddled sheep
    Are like white clouds upon the grass,
And merry herdsmen guard their sleep
    And chat and watch the big stars pass.

It is a pleasant thing to lie
    Upon the meadow on the hill
With kindly fellowship near by
    Of sheep and men of gentle will.

I lean upon my broken crook
    And dream of sheep and grass and men—
O shameful eyes that cannot look
    On any honest thing again!

On bloody feet I clambered down
    And fled the wages of my sin,
I am the leavings of the town,
    And meanly serve its meanest inn.

THE FOURTH SHEPHERD (continued)

I tramp the courtyard stones in grief,
　　While sleep takes man and beast to her.
And every cloud is calling "Thief!"
　　And every star calls "Murderer!"

THE FOURTH SHEPHERD (continued)

II

The hand of God is sure and strong,
   Nor shall a man forever flee
The bitter punishment of wrong.
   The wrath of God is over me!

With ashen bread and wine of tears
   Shall I be solaced in my pain.
I wear through black and endless years
   Upon my brow the mark of Cain.

THE FOURTH SHEPHERD (continued)

III

Poor vagabond, so old and mild,
  Will they not keep him for a night?
And She, a woman great with child,
  So frail and pitiful and white.

Good people, since the tavern door
  Is shut to you, come here instead.
See, I have cleansed my stable floor
  And piled fresh hay to make a bed.

Here is some milk and oaten cake.
  Lie down and sleep and rest you fair,
Nor fear, O simple folk, to take
  The bounty of a child of care.

THE FOURTH SHEPHERD (continued)

IV

On nights like this the huddled sheep—
   I never saw a night so fair.
How huge the sky is, and how deep!
   And how the planets flash and glare!

At dawn beside my drowsy flock
   What wingéd music I have heard!
But now the clouds with singing rock
   As if the sky were turning bird.

O blinding Light, O blinding Light!
   Burn through my heart with sweetest pain.
O flaming Song, most loudly bright,
   Consume away my deadly stain!

THE FOURTH SHEPHERD (continued)

V

The stable glows against the sky,
  And who are these that throng the way?
My three old comrades hasten by
  And shining angels kneel and pray.

The door swings wide—I cannot go—
  I must and yet I dare not see.
Lord, who am I that I should know—
  Lord, God, be merciful to me!

THE FOURTH SHEPHERD (continued)

VI

O Whiteness, whiter than the fleece
  Of new-washed sheep on April sod!
O Breath of Life, O Prince of Peace,
  O Lamb of God, O Lamb of God!

EASTER

THE air is like a butterfly
        With frail blue wings.
The happy earth looks at the sky
    And sings.

MOUNT HOUVENKOPF

SERENE he stands, with mist serenely
   crowned,
   And draws a cloak of trees about his breast.
   The thunder roars but cannot break his rest
And from his rugged face the tempests bound.
He does not heed the angry lightning's wound,
   The raging blizzard is his harmless guest,
   And human life is but a passing jest
To him who sees Time spin the years around.

But fragile souls, in skyey reaches find
   High vantage-points and view him from afar.
How low he seems to the ascended mind,
   How brief he seems where all things endless
      are;
This little playmate of the mighty wind
   This young companion of an ancient star.

THE HOUSE WITH NOBODY IN IT

WHENEVER I walk to Suffern along the
Erie track
I go by a poor old farmhouse with its shingles
broken and black.
I suppose I've passed it a hundred times, but I
always stop for a minute
And look at the house, the tragic house, the
house with nobody in it.

I never have seen a haunted house, but I hear
there are such things;
That they hold the talk of spirits, their mirth
and sorrowings.
I know this house isn't haunted, and I wish it
were, I do;
For it wouldn't be so lonely if it had a ghost or
two.

This house on the road to Suffern needs a dozen
panes of glass,
And somebody ought to weed the walk and take
a scythe to the grass.

THE HOUSE WITH NOBODY IN IT (cont.)

It needs new paint and shingles, and the vines
    should be trimmed and tied;
But what it needs the most of all is some people
    living inside.

If I had a lot of money and all my debts were
    paid
I'd put a gang of men to work with brush and
    saw and spade.
I'd buy that place and fix it up the way it used
    to be
And I'd find some people who wanted a home and
    give it to them free.

Now, a new house standing empty, with staring
    window and door,
Looks idle, perhaps, and foolish, like a hat on
    its block in the store.
But there's nothing mournful about it; it can-
    not be sad and lone
For the lack of something within it that it has
    never known.

THE HOUSE WITH NOBODY IN IT (cont.)

But a house that has done what a house should
    do, a house that has sheltered life,
That has put its loving wooden arms around a
    man and his wife,
A house that has echoed a baby's laugh and held
    up his stumbling feet,
Is the saddest sight, when it's left alone, that ever
    your eyes could meet.

So whenever I go to Suffern along the Erie track
I never go by the empty house without stopping
    and looking back,
Yet it hurts me to look at the crumbling roof
    and the shutters fallen apart,
For I can't help thinking the poor old house is
    a house with a broken heart.

DAVE LILLY

THERE'S a brook on the side of Greylock
    that used to be full of trout,
But there's nothing there now but minnows;
    they say it is all fished out.
I fished there many a Summer day some twenty
    years ago,
And I never quit without getting a mess of a
    dozen or so.

There was a man, Dave Lilly, who lived on the
    North Adams road,
And he spent all his time fishing, while his neigh-
    bors reaped and sowed.
He was the luckiest fisherman in the Berkshire
    hills, I think.
And when he didn't go fishing he'd sit in the
    tavern and drink.

Well, Dave is dead and buried and nobody cares
    very much;
They have no use in Greylock for drunkards and
    loafers and such.

DAVE LILLY (continued)

But I always liked Dave Lilly, he was pleasant
    as you could wish;
He was shiftless and good-for-nothing, but he
    certainly could fish.

The other night I was walking up the hill from
    Williamstown
And I came to the brook I mentioned, and I
    stopped on the bridge and sat down.
I looked at the blackened water with its little
    flecks of white
And I heard it ripple and whisper in the still of
    the Summer night.

And after I'd been there a minute it seemed to
    me I could feel
The presence of someone near me, and I heard
    the hum of a reel.
And the water was churned and broken, and
    something was brought to land
By a twist and flirt of a shadowy rod in a deft
    and shadowy hand.

DAVE LILLY (continued)

I scrambled down to the brookside and hunted
 all about;
There wasn't a sign of a fisherman; there wasn't
 a sign of a trout.
But I heard somebody chuckle behind the hol-
 low oak
And I got a whiff of tobacco like Lilly used to
 smoke.

It's fifteen years, they tell me, since anyone fished
 that brook;
And there's nothing in it but minnows that nib-
 ble the bait off your hook.
But before the sun has risen and after the moon
 has set
I know that it's full of ghostly trout for Lilly's
 ghost to get.

I guess I'll go to the tavern and get a bottle of
 rye
And leave it down by the hollow oak, where
 Lilly's ghost went by.

DAVE LILLY (continued)

I meant to go up on the hillside and try to find
    his grave
And put some flowers on it—but this will be bet-
    ter for Dave.

ALARM CLOCKS

WHEN Dawn strides out to wake a dewy
        farm
  Across green fields and yellow hills of hay
  The little twittering birds laugh in his way
And poise triumphant on his shining arm.
He bears a sword of flame but not to harm
  The wakened life that feels his quickening
        sway
  And barnyard voices shrilling "It is day!"
Take by his grace a new and alien charm.

But in the city, like a wounded thing
  That limps to cover from the angry chase,
He steals down streets where sickly arc-lights
        sing,
  And wanly mock his young and shameful face;
And tiny gongs with cruel fervor ring
  In many a high and dreary sleeping place.

WAVERLEY

1814-1914

WHEN, on a novel's newly printed page
  We find a maudlin eulogy of sin,
And read of ways that harlots wander in,
And of sick souls that writhe in helpless rage;
Or when Romance, bespectacled and sage,
  Taps on her desk and bids the class begin
  To con the problems that have always been
Perplexed mankind's unhappy heritage;

Then in what robes of honor habited
  The laureled wizard of the North appears!
Who raised Prince Charlie's cohorts from the
    dead,
  Made Rose's mirth and Flora's noble tears,
And formed that shining legion at whose head
  Rides Waverley, triumphant o'er the years!

THE PEACEMAKER

UPON his will he binds a radiant chain
　　For Freedom's sake he is no longer free
It is his task, the slave of Liberty
With his own blood to wash away a stain.
That pain may cease, he yields his flesh to pain
To banish war he must a warrior be
He dwells in night Eternal Dawn to see
And gladly dies abundant life to gain.

What matters Death, if Freedom be not dead?
No flags are fair if Freedom's flag be furled
Who fights for Freedom goes with joyful tread
To meet the fires of Hell against him hurled.
And has for Captain Him Whose thorn-crowned head
Smiles from the Cross upon a conquered world.

　　　　　　　　　　　Joyce Kilmer

France, June 14, 1918.

*This is the last poem written by Joyce Kilmer, a week
before his death in France in June 1918. The original
copy was sent to the Reverend Francis P. Duffy,
Chaplain of the Fighting 69th Regiment.*

Candles That Burn

BY ALINE KILMER

Cherokee Publishing Company
Atlanta, Georgia

Library of Congress Cataloging-in-Publication Data

Kilmer, Aline, 1888–1941.
    Candles that burn / by Aline Kilmer.
        p.   cm.
    ISBN: 0-87797-267-2 : $14.95
    I. Title
PS3521.I37C3   1994
811'.54--dc20

This book is printed on acid-free paper which conforms to the American National Standard Z39.48-1984 *Permanence of Paper for Printed Library Materials*. Paper that conforms to this standard's requirements for pH, alkaline reserve and freedom from ground-wood is anticipated to last several hundred years without significant deterioration under normal library use and storage conditions. ∞

Manufactured in the United States of America

ISBN: 0-87797-267-2

 Cherokee Publishing Company
P O Box 1730, Marietta, Ga 30061

CONTENTS

CONTENTS

CANDLES THAT BURN

AMBITION

Kenton and Deborah, Michael and Rose,
These are fine children as all the world knows;
But into my arms in my dreams every night
Come Peter and Christopher, Faith and Delight.

Kenton is tropical, Rose is pure white,
Deborah shines like a star in the night;
Michael's round eyes are as blue as the sea,
And nothing on earth could be dearer to me.

But where is the baby with Faith can compare?
What is the colour of Peterkin's hair?
Who can make Christopher clear to my sight,
Or show me the eyes of my daughter Delight?

When people inquire I always just state:
"I have four nice children and hope to have eight.
Though the first four are pretty and certain to please,
Who knows but the rest may be nicer than these?"

THE MOTHER'S HELPER

I love all my children far more than I thought to;
They do everything just the way that they ought to,
And the ones that can talk say their prayers as they're
    taught to;
But still every night as I sit at my sewing,
My mind turned adrift on its own pleasures going,
Underneath my wild thoughts is a steady prayer flowing:
      St. Brigid, please keep
      My babies asleep!

St. Rita assists me when things are past bearing,
St. Christopher helps me when forth I am faring,
But the care of my children St. Brigid is sharing.
They are wilful and happy and dear beyond measure,
No riches could equal the worth of my treasure;
But in spite of my love and my pride and my pleasure,
      St. Brigid, please keep
      My babies asleep!

A DIDACTIC POEM TO DEBORAH

Deborah dear, when you are old,
  Tired and grey, with pallid brow,
Where will you put the blue and gold
  And radiant rose that tint you now?

You are so fair, so gay, so sweet!
  How can I bear to watch you grow,
Knowing that soon those twinkling feet
  Must go the ways all children go?

Deborah, put the blue and gold
  And rosy beauty that is you,
Into your heart that it may hold
  Beauty to last your whole life through.

Then, though the world be tossed and torn,
  Greyer than ashes and as sad,
Though fate may make your way forlorn,
  Deborah dear, you shall be glad.

AN AUTUMN WALK WITH DEBORAH

Over the limp and sallow grasses,
  Deborah, will you walk with me?
You may gather gentians in purple masses
  And honeypods from the locust tree.

Brown leaves cover the partridge berry,
  Holding it safe for your eager hand.
Barberry bright and cornelian cherry
  Offering scarlet jewels stand.

I shall dress you up as an elf-queen, twining
  Bittersweet wreaths for your golden head;
Your leaf-brown cloak with its orange lining
  I shall hang with garlands yellow and red.

Let us leave this place while the sunlight lingers
  Lest the elves should covet your beauty bright.
The gentians fall from your tired fingers
  As I carry you home through the fading light.

EXPERIENCE

Deborah danced, when she was two,
As buttercups and daffodils do;
Spirited, frail, naïvely bold,
Her hair a ruffled crest of gold,
And whenever she spoke her voice went singing
Like water up from a fountain springing.

But now her step is quiet and slow;
She walks the way primroses go;
Her hair is yellow instead of gilt,
Her voice is losing its lovely lilt,
And in place of her wild, delightful ways
A quaint precision rules her days.

For Deborah now is three, and oh,
She knows so much that she did not know.

CANDLES THAT BURN

Candles that burn for a November birthday,
  Wreathed round with asters and with goldenrod,
As you go upward in your radiant dying
  Carry my prayer to God.

Tell Him she is so small and so rebellious,
  Tell Him her words are music on her lips,
Tell Him I love her in her wayward beauty
  Down to her fingertips.

Ask Him to keep her brave and true and lovely,
  Vivid and happy, gay as she is now,
Ask Him to let no shadow touch her beauty,
  No sorrow mar her brow.

All the sweet saints that came for her baptising,
  Tell them I pray them to be always near.
Ask them to keep her little feet from stumbling,
  Her gallant heart from fear.

Candles that burn for a November birthday,
  Wreathed round with asters and with goldenrod,
As you go upward in your radiant dying,
  Carry my prayer to God.

PREVISION

I know you are too dear to stay;
　　You are so exquisitely sweet:
My lonely house will thrill some day
　　To echoes of your eager feet.

I hold your words within my heart,
　　So few, so infinitely dear;
Watching your fluttering hands I start
　　At the corroding touch of fear.

A faint, unearthly music rings
　　From you to Heaven—it is not far!
A mist about your beauty clings
　　Like a thin cloud before a star.

My heart shall keep the child I knew,
　　When you are really gone from me,
And spend its life remembering you
　　As shells remember the lost sea.

DOROTHY'S GARDEN

Dear, in all your garden I have planted yellow lilies,
  Dainty yellow lilies everywhere you go:
They are nodding slim and stately down the paths along
    the hedges,
  Delicately stepping they curtsey in a row.

So when you walk among them like a lily in your slim-
    ness,
  With your shining head just bending graciously,
All the little angels that look down upon your garden
  Will wonder which is lily and which is Dorothy.

JUSTICE

Michael, come in! Stop crying at the door.
  Come in and see the evil you have done.
  Here is your sister's doll with one leg gone,
Naked and helpless on the playroom floor.
"Poor child! poor child! now he can never stand.
  With one leg less he could not even sit!"
She mourned, but first, with swift avenging hand,
  She smote, and I am proud of her for it.

Michael, my sympathies are all for you.
  Your cherub mouth, your miserable eyes,
  Your grey-blue smock tear-spattered and your cries
Shatter my heart, but what am I to do?
He was her baby and the fear of bears
  Lay heavy on him so he could not sleep
But in the crook of her dear arm, she swears.
  So, Michael, she was right and you must weep.

FOR TWO BIRTHDAYS

Whenever I light the candles for your birthday
  My memory lights two more,
Two ghostly candles burning with your candles
  Where hers burned once before.

Whenever I see you at your birthday table,
  Across from you I see
A gentle ghost that sits among us laughing,
  Laughing adorably.

She would have been the gayest at the party,
  She always was the gladdest thing on earth:
Now she is gayer still, for she is taken
  Into celestial mirth.

With God and all the saints and all the angels
  She shares her birthday cake.
So let us keep your birthday candles burning
  Joyously, for her sake.

TO ROSE AWAY

Little white moon of my heart
   Since you have gone away
I miss your cry when you wake by night,
   Your smile when you wake by day.
I am glad when the daylight fades
   For my dreams are lovely things;
Then in the dark you come to me
   On softly fluttering wings.

When in the afternoon,
   Sailing the cloudless sky,
Over the shimmering summer earth
   The pale little moon slips by,
In the curve of her frail white bow
   Your shadowy face I see,
And I like to think that she has you there
   Bringing you back to me.

FOR A PROUD BABY

Flower of children, if you knew
　All the things you *might* be proud of!
Curls and dimples are a few
　Charms you have a gracious crowd of.

With your dark, delightful eyes
　You can break a heart or mend it.
I know you are not really wise,
　But how well you can pretend it!

Though your wickedness and wit
　Very clever in your sight be,
Yet you are not, I admit,
　As conceited as you might be.

"YOU ARE MORE BLESSED"

You are more blessed than other babies are:
  Your shining eyes grow brighter every day
With radiance that reminds me of the star
  That showed where Jesus lay.

I like to think that you are set apart,
  A flower that never sprang from earthly loam,
A rose of Heaven that nestles in my heart
  And dreams about its home.

TO A SICK CHILD

I would make you cookies
    But you could not eat them;
I would bring you roses
    But you would not care.
In your scornful beauty,
    Arrogant and patient,
Though I'd die to please you
    You lie silent there.

Your once wanton sister
    Creeps about on tiptoe,
And your brother hurries
    At your slightest nod:
Watching at your bedside
    When you sleep I tremble
Lest before you waken
    You go back to God.

"A WIND IN THE NIGHT"

A wind rose in the night,
  (She had always feared it so!)
Sorrow plucked at my heart
  And I could not help but go.

Softly I went and stood
  By her door at the end of the hall.
Dazed with grief I watched
  The candles flaring and tall.

The wind was wailing aloud:
  I thought how she would have cried
For my warm familiar arms
  And the sense of me by her side.

The candles flickered and leapt,
  The shadows jumped on the wall.
She lay before me small and still
  And did not care at all.

"WHEN YOU HAD BEEN DEAD"

When you had been dead a week
I entered a shining shop,
And there in a neat pink row
Lay little dolls made of soap.
And I thought, "I will take one home.
How she will laugh to see it!
How it will bob in her bath
And slip through her dripping fingers!"
Only a moment I smiled.
Only a moment I dreamed it.
Then my heart stood still with pain
And I went out into the darkness.

TO ROSE

They told me the one who died would be always near me,
   That I had one child who could never grow old and
      sad;
I should always have your beautiful face to cheer me,
   Your voice to make me glad.

Oh, I have prayed till my heart was weary with praying,
   Hoping, if only in dreams, to feel you near,
To find the truth in what they were always saying—
   That you would be with me, dear.

Were they only trying to help me face the morrow?
   Or did they really believe the things they said?
The only dream I have had of you brought but sorrow:
   I dreamed that you were not dead.

OLIM MEMINISSE JUVABIT

Sometime it may be pleasing to remember
   The curls about your brow,
To talk about your eyes, your smile, your dearness,
   But it is anguish now.

Often I feel that I must speak and tell them
   Of all your golden ways,
How all the words you ever spoke were happy,
   Joy-filled your laughing days.

But though I miss you every empty moment
   Of all my longing years,
How can I speak about your thrilling beauty
   When all my thoughts are tears?

Sometime it may be pleasing to remember
   The curls about your brow,
The way you turned your head, your hands, your
    laughter,
   But oh, not now, not now!

HAUNTED

Your dying lips were proud and sweet
And when you turned your head away
Against the pillow where you lay
My heart was broken at your feet.
O quivering lips that would be gay,
What was it that you tried to say?
There was a thing you would have said,
There was a word you never spoke;
It rose between us by your bed.
There came a look of hurt surprise
In your unfathomable eyes,
And then it was that my heart broke.

So now wherever I may turn
I see your wistful, following eyes;
I see that anguished question burn
On lips that laugh in Paradise.
If I had been in your dear place
You never would have failed me so!
You always read upon my face

Thoughts that myself could scarcely know.
Oh, how I scorned my fettered soul
Because it could not leap the space
That held me from your lovely goal!

How many a trivial little word
And things you said to me apart,
Strange sayings no one else has heard,
I keep safe buried in my heart.
But the last thing you would have said,
I shall not know it: you are dead.

THE WINDY NIGHT

You say you love to hear the wind
    Like brazen trumpets in the night;
That all its martial panoply
    Wakes in your soul a wild delight.

You like to hear upon the roof
    The silver lances of the rain,
And see the birches' cavalry
    Go sweeping past the window-pane:

To see tall chestnuts fall like towers,
    While all our happy house is still,
And like a charge with bayonets
    The cedar trees rush up the hill.

But I lie trembling in the night,
    As dark and wild as night can be,
Remembering songs that you have made
    Till through the night you come to me.

I SHALL NOT BE AFRAID

I shall not be afraid any more,
    Either by night or day;
What would it profit me to be afraid
    With you away?

Now I am brave.   In the dark night alone
    All through the house I go,
Locking the doors and making windows fast
    When sharp winds blow.

For there is only sorrow in my heart;
    There is no room for fear.
But how I wish I were afraid again,
    My dear, my dear!

IN SPRING

I do not know which is worse when you are away:
  Long grey days with the lisping sound of the rain
And then when the lilac dusk is beginning to fall
    The thought that perhaps you may never come back
    again;

Or days when the world is a shimmer of blue and gold,
  Sparkling newly all in the dear spring weather,
When with a heart that is torn apart by pain
  I walk alone in ways that we went together.

HIGH HEART

The sea that I watch from my window
Is grey and white;
I see it toss in the darkness
All the night.
My soul swoops down to sorrow
As the sea-gulls dip,
And all my love flies after
Your lonely ship.

Yet I am not despairing
Though we must part,
Nothing can be too bitter
For my high heart.
All in the dreary midnight,
Watching the flying foam,
I wait for the golden morning
When you come home.

CHRISTMAS

"And shall you have a Tree," they say,
"Now one is dead and one away?"

Oh, I shall have a Christmas Tree!
Brighter than ever it shall be;
Dressed out with coloured lights to make
The room all glorious for your sake.
And under the Tree a Child shall sleep
Near shepherds watching their wooden sheep.
Threads of silver and nets of gold,
Scarlet bubbles the Tree shall hold,
And little glass bells that tinkle clear.
I shall trim it alone but feel you near.

And when Christmas Day is almost done,
When they all grow sleepy one by one,
When Kenton's books have all been read,
When Deborah's climbing the stairs to bed,

I shall sit alone by the fire and see
Ghosts of you both come close to me.
For the dead and the absent always stay
With the one they love on Christmas Day.

THE GARDEN CHILD

Once in my childhood I knew an old garden,
    Shut in by grey pickets and crowded with grass;
Old flowers grew in it, clove pinks and white lilies,
    And moss roses choked up the path with their mass.

It lay all alone in the curve of a river
    Where little grey boats floated by on the tide;
No dwelling was near it, no pathway led to it,
    And harsh river-grasses crept up on each side.

Speedwell and lavender, small brown chrysanthemums,
    Mixed in great tangles where myrtle ran wild,
And sweetly mysterious, safe though unguarded,
    Lay hid in a corner the grave of a child.

Often I wondered if that child had played there,
    Played there as I, twining wreaths for my hair,
When the pickets were white and the flowers were tended
    And no little grave held its mystery there.

Who were the people who once had lived near there
    Making the wilderness bloom like a rose,
Then left like a dream leaving nothing behind them
    But the grave of a child in a small garden-close?

THE LOST FOREST

I walked with my mother
  Where the tall trees grow,
And she showed me tiny tables
  Where the elves sit in a row,
And the bells that ring to call them
  When the night winds blow.

There were small frosted toadstools,
  And little cups of wine,
And velvet banks to rest on
  Where moss grew thick and fine,
And a smooth brown ring for dancing
  Underneath a pine.

But now when I go walking
  All the way is clear;
The little bells are silent
  And the moss grown sere,
And I know that in the moonlight
  Not an elf comes near.

COW SONG

Klang! Kling! the cow-bells ring
  As the cows come home at night.
Slowly they pass over the grass,
  Black and brown and white.

Sleepy and slow each one will go
  With daisies and clover in her;
At the milking stall she'll give them all
  As milk for Kenton's dinner.

REMEMBRANCE

I went back to a place I knew
    When I was very, very small;
The same old yellow roses grew
    Against the same old wall.

Each thing I knew was in its place;
    The well, the white stones by the road,
The box-hedge with its cobweb lace,
    And a small spotted toad.

And yet the place seemed changed and still;
    The house itself had shrunk, I know.
And then my eyes began to fill—
    For I had always loved it so!

FLOWER DANCERS

To-day I played with flowers,
The yellow, yellow daisies,
The rainbow morning-glories
  And lilies pale and grand.
They held their dainty skirts out,
They bowed among the grasses,
And danced a tilting minuet
  Shadowy hand in hand.

MORNING-GLORIES

When I was small I used to play
   In an old garden bright with flowers.
I often used to run away
   From home, and play in there for hours.

There were two ladies who lived there,
   Dressed all in black with creamy laces.
They had soft snowy puffs of hair
   And wrinkled, pleasant, dim old faces.

They had such kind and pretty ways!
   They used to tell me lovely stories,
And let me on warm sunny days
   Blow bubbles with great morning-glories.

I wonder if they know how much
   I think of them now I am older.
I often seem to feel the touch
   Of soft old hands upon my shoulder.

HILL-COUNTRY

Brown hill I have left behind,
   Why do you haunt me so?
You never were warm and kind
   And I was glad to go.

Is it because there lies,
   Up in your cold brown breast,
One who brought joy to my eyes
   And to my heart brought rest?

Never again shall I see
   The flash in her answering eye.
Never again shall the heart in me
   Stir as she passes by.

Hill, you are proud and cold,
   Haughty and high your face;
Is it, O hill, because you hold
   Her in your grim embrace?

COMPENSATION

I have two children: one who came
   When on my head
Life shed its joys without a thought
   Of pain or dread;
And one when ashes of despair
   Blackened my bread.

My child of joy has sombre eyes
   Like Mimer's well;
Surely the secrets of the world
   Those lips could tell;
And wisdom on his infant soul
   Untimely fell.

My child of woe has laughing eyes
   Like dancing light;
A leaping flame of innocence
   Has burned her white;
And in her face I dare not look,
   It is so bright.

My little pagan's life should hold
   Joy without taint;
Under the gleaming sword of pain
   His soul might faint:
Not all the powers of Hell could daunt
   My happy saint!

IN A HALL BEDROOM

"In the long border on the right
  I shall plant larkspur first," she thinks.
"Peonies and chrysanthemums
  And then sweet-scented maiden pinks.

"The border on the left shall hold
  Nothing but masses of white phlox.
Forget-me-nots shall edge this one,
  The one across be edged with box.

"The sun-dial in the centre stands.
  There morning-glories bright shall twine.
And in the strip at either end
  Shall grow great clumps of columbine.

"There is no garden in the world
  So beautiful as mine," she dreams.
Rising, she walks the little space
  To where her narrow window gleams.

She gazes through the dingy pane
    To where the street is noisy still,
And tends with pitiable care
    A tulip on the window-sill.

TO A YOUNG AVIATOR

When you go up to die
  Some not far distant day,
I wonder will you try
  To tear your mask away,
    And look life in the eyes
    For once without disguise?

Behind your mask may hide
  What treacherous, covered fires!
What hidden, torturing pride!
  What sorrows, what desires!
    Whatever there may be
    There will be none to see.

Yet I think when you meet
  Death coming through the skies,
Calmly his face you'll greet,
  Coldly, without surprise;
    Then die without a moan,
    Still masked although alone.

THE MASQUERADER

You were no more to me than many others,
  I never thought you beautiful or bright,
And yet I find your memory returning
  Many a night.

Again I hear your strange, heart-broken laughter,
  Laughter more pitiful than any tears;
Again I see your gallant head uplifted
  Through heavy years.

You held so tight the fragile toy you wanted,
  And when it broke you would not let it go;
You would not let us guess your heart broke with it—
  You played you did not know.

Now you are gone we see how well you suffered,
  We see the valiant way you struggled on.
Can you forgive our foolish condescension,
  Now you are gone?

THE MORNING SHADOW

I who have never known sorrow
Wait for it morning and evening;
For the footstep of grief on my threshold,
The drip of tears on my hearthstone,
The pitiless hours of lonely, uncomforted woe.

Never a life without sorrow!
But, oh, when will mine be upon me?
When will the years seem long
That now slip happily by me?
The light of the skies be dimmed
To eyes that are weary with weeping?

AFTER GRIEVING

When I was young I was so sad!
  I was so sad! I did not know
Why any living thing was glad
  Vhen one must some day sorrow so.
    But now that grief has come to me
    My heart is like a bird set free.

I always knew that it would come;
  I always felt it waiting there:
Its shadow kept my glad voice dumb
  And crushed my gay soul with despair.
    But now that I have lived with grief
    I feel an exquisite relief.

Athletes who know their proven strength,
  Ships that have shamed the hurricane:
These are my brothers, and at length
  I shall come back to joy again.
    However hard my life may be
    I know it shall not conquer me.

SPRING SORROW

Sorrow to see the spring!
Why do we smile when she wakes the rose?
For sleep is sweeter as every one knows,
And cruel the wakening.

Hark to a weary sound!
It is the sap that swells like tears
In the heart of trees that are grey with years,
And falls like tears to the ground.

Futile the brave display,
The pitiful challenge of bud and leaf,
The proud pretence that is yet so brief
And dies, like spring, in a day.

Sorrow to see the spring!
Why are we glad at the birth of the rose?
For death is better as every one knows,
And life is a bitter thing.

AGE INVADING

I shall not run upstairs again,
  And oh, the foolish grief I feel!
I must go carefully or pain
  Will thrust me through with its bright steel.

I never thought that I should care
  When the first shadow fell on me.
I planned lace caps for my white hair
  And hoped to grow old gracefully.

I thought that when Age came I'd stand
  (If Age should really come at all!)
And greet him with extended hand
  As my last partner at a ball.

But now when you with easy grace
  Run up ahead or wait for me,
Such bitterness is in my face
  I turn my head lest you should see.

PORTRAIT OF AN OLD LADY

Early one morning as I went a-walking
  I met an old lady so stately and tall,
The red of her cheeks gave a quiver of pleasure
  Like the sight of red hollyhocks by a grey wall.

Fragrance of lavender clung to her, telling
  Of linen piled high on immaculate shelves;
You could fancy her tending her garden or strolling
  Among the proud roses that grow by themselves.

When I am sorrowful, dreading the future,
  Dreaming of days when my hair shall be grey,
It cheers me to think of that lovely old lady,
  Lavender-haunted and hollyhock-gay.

TO TWO LITTLE SISTERS OF THE POOR

Sweet and humble and gladly poor,
The Grace of God came in at my door.

Sorrow and death were mine that day,
But the Grace of God came in to stay;

The Grace of God that spread its wings
Over all sad and pitiful things.

Sorrow turned to the touch of God,
Death became but His welcoming nod.

Grey-eyed, comforting, strong and brave,
You came to ask but instead you gave.

Quickly you came and went, you two,
But the Grace of God stayed after you.

MOUNTAINS

Over the green and level land
  My sad eyes wander without hope;
Here no rejoicing mountains stand,
  No strong and friendly slope.

But ever when I close my eyes
  Tall mountains rear their stately forms.
Against the sky I watch them rise,
  Serene in calm or storms.

One in the distance rises blue,
  Haloed by morning's earliest beams.
This was the peak my childhood knew,
  About her clung my dreams.

Over her pallor fell the snow,
  The hot sun scorched her fertile breast,
But in the summer lightning's glow
  I always loved her best.

She bowed her purple head in pain
   As clouds rolled up from threatening space,
And let a veil of silver rain
   Slip down across her weeping face.

TO A LADY COMPLIMENTING

When I met you an hour ago
   My heart was heavy and chill;
Now, from your word of praise,
   It is glowing still.

Ah, *vanitas vanitatum!*
   What the Preacher said was true!
I always thought my eyes were grey
   But now I know they are blue.

GREEN GRAVEL

Fidelia goes sadly and sits in the door;
She spins or she stares at the white sanded floor.
She has never a visitor all the day long,
And she sings very softly this foolish old song:

"*Green Gravel, Green Gravel, your grass is so green!*
The sweetest, the sweetest that ever was seen!
Fidelia, Fidelia, your sweetheart is dead;
He sent you this letter to turn back your head."

But when it is evening she wanders away
And watches the children who come out to play.
The children are happy, they dance in a ring,
And over and over they merrily sing:

"*Green Gravel, Green Gravel, your grass is so green!*
The sweetest, the sweetest that ever was seen!"
She wants to sing with them and join in their fun
But when she comes near them away they all run.

So late in the evening she dances alone
And sings rather drearily round a white stone:
"Fidelia, Fidelia, your sweetheart is dead;
He sent you this letter to turn back your head."

THE WHITE MOTH

Where are you flying, White Moth, to-night,
  Bearing a pale little soul away,
A sad little soul that quivers with fright
  As the moonbeams over your frail wings play?

Peace! I conjure you, fly no more,
  Come no nearer the beckoning flame.
Wan little soul from an unknown shore,
  Not by chance to my light you came.

Somewhere I have known your silver wings,
  Somewhere I have thrilled to your lonely flight.
I am sad with the ache of forgotten things;
  Leave me alone in peace to-night.

HONEY-WITCH

Gay Peter rode by the grey tower
   And a face leaned laughing down,
With hair that gleamed from a gold net
   And eyes of angel-brown.
"She is fair," he said as he saw her,
   "Tender and good and gay.
So pure that I am all unworthy,"
   And sighing he rode away.

Gay Peter married a good maid
   Because of her bold blue eyes,
But ever he dreamed of the lady
   Pure as the frosty skies.
Everywhere he wandered
   He thought of a heart-shaped face
Set like a star in a dark sky
   As his soul's abiding place.

But up in her tower the lady
   Bit her honey-coloured hands and cried:
"Shall I never get out of the grey tower?
   Shall I never get out?" she sighed.

But no one guessed who passed there
  That her goodness all was lies,
That she had the heart of a honey-witch
  Behind her angel eyes.

TO A SILLY POOR SOUL

"If ever thou gavest meat or drink,
  Every nighte and alle;
The fire shall never make thee shrink,
  And Christe receive thy saule."

For meat and drink that you have given
God will find you a place in Heaven.

For the kind words that you have spoken
God will not let your soul be broken.

Bread on the waters you have cast
And God will save your soul at last.

Wherever you go—and the world is wide—
My prayers shall be ever at your side.

For I, perverse and foolish, too,
Know the dark ways your soul went through.

You who were given the greatest grace
Cast it away with a tortured face.

But if I see the good in you
Will God in His mercy not see it, too?

Will God not make you clean and whole
And Christ receive your silly poor soul?

MOONLIGHT

The moon reached in cold hands across the sill
    And touched me as I lay sleeping;
And in my sleep I thought of sorrowful things:
    I wakened, and I lay weeping.

I could hear on the beach below the small waves break
    And fall on the silver shingle,
And the sound of a footstep passing in the street
    Where lamplight and moonlight mingle.

And I said: "All day I can turn my face to the sun
    And lead my thoughts to laughter;
But I hope in my heart that I never shall sleep again
    Because of the pain thereafter."

The moon's pale fingers wandered across my face
    And the arm where my hot cheek rested,
And because of the tears in my eyes I could not see
    Where the black waves rocked moon-crested.

MY MIRROR

There is a mirror in my room
Less like a mirror than a tomb,
There are so many ghosts that pass
Across the surface of the glass.

When in the morning I arise
With circles round my tired eyes,
Seeking the glass to brush my hair
My mother's mother meets me there.

If in the middle of the day
I happen to go by that way,
I see a smile I used to know—
My mother, twenty years ago.

But when I rise by candlelight
To feed my baby in the night,
Then whitely in the glass I see
My dead child's face look out at me.